S0-BHS-145

language of home

the interiors of foley & cox

language of home

the interiors of foley & cox

MICHAEL COX

FOREWORD BY PAMELA JACCARINO

ℳ

preface

Twenty years ago, we established Foley & Cox with the goal of improving the quality of life through timeless, elegant interiors. For the past two decades, the firm has been privileged to work with discerning clients to interpret their vision for homes all over the world. We have cultivated long-term, personal relationships with them, and many return to commission work for second and third residences and some for their now-grown children. We have also developed rewarding partnerships with talented residential architecture, landscape architecture, and building firms as well as the artisans who transform their interiors.

Founding partner Mary Foley and I met and worked together as a design team at Ralph Lauren and then embraced our entrepreneurial spirits and talents to establish Foley & Cox in 2002. Upon Mary's retirement, the firm transitioned to a team of executives and designers who create beautiful environments to address the personal and practical needs and aesthetic dreams of our clients and translate them into relevant interiors for today.

Each collaboration has been an opportunity to flex our creative muscles, interpret our clients' desires, draw inspiration from the history of design, and learn from the incredible artisans and craftspeople we partner with.

Lessons learned and principles developed along the way:

- Listen to the clients and take copious notes.
- Seek input from artists and craftspeople.
- Plan ahead—then think further ahead.
- Respect all involved—both collaborators and doormen.
- Be willing to compromise but defend your vision passionately.
- Understand that design is truly in the details and the smallest repurpose of memorabilia draws the largest smile.

A generation is defined by a twenty-year time period, and we have slowly and carefully molded our firm's vision: Timeless, elegant, bespoke—the language of Foley & Cox.

MICHAEL COX
Fall 2022

foreword

Our lunch was scheduled for one o'clock, and just prior to the top of the hour, in walked Michael Cox. Smartly dressed, and with a warm and welcoming smile, he slid into the booth across from me, leaned forward, and thus we began the first of many engaging conversations about design. Michael chatted about his firm and spoke of the pleasure he derives from gathering creative clues and inspiration to establish the tone, the mood, the romance of a project.

Michael Cox has spent the last twenty years creating a body of work that is tailored, stylish, and enduring. Step through the front door of any home his firm has designed, and you get it. The rooms are fresh, never fusty. The art pops, the furnishings beckon, and the spirit of the home emerges. His craft, and that of his partner, Mary Foley, who has since retired, was honed at Ralph Lauren. Ralph made everything about integrity, effortless ease, and style—with rigorous attention to detail. Unsurprisingly, therefore, Michael's own work is timeless, bespoke, and beautifully executed.

Through the years, we had the great pleasure of publishing Michael's design projects in *Luxe Interiors + Design*. His thoughtfulness and careful attention are evident in the work. A modern family compound in Southampton is one of my favorites. Punctuated with bold and visually impactful moments and an art collection ripe with creative expression, the home is quintessential Foley & Cox in its crisp take on a classic. Michael's gift for eclecticism shines brightly in another project that graced our pages. A distinguished prewar Park Avenue apartment for a young family who wanted to inject a downtown vibe required a deft hand and sensitive balancing act. Michael and Mary layered a mix of antiques and contemporary pieces and a blend of eras and styles that read light and renewed. When we are selecting projects for publication, we often ask ourselves how the spaces make us feel. The word that comes to mind when thinking about Foley & Cox projects is ... delight.

As you browse through the pages of *Language of Home,* you will discover the firm to be well versed in the vernacular they have refined. Michael often mentions that clients seek out his firm to interpret their vision. I believe it is also the graceful dialogue of design that attracts them. Foley & Cox speaks in a welcoming and serene voice, with a deference to natural light, a spirit of optimism, and a focus on comfort and felicity. When asked to describe his style, Michael told me it is about "appropriateness." He always asks, "What drives the design on this project? Where is it? Who is the client? What's their lifestyle? All of this will determine the design."

Finally, this beautiful book is a love letter of sorts, from Michael and his team, and dedicated to those who have enriched and informed the firm's work—from longstanding clients, "patrons of the creative arts," as he refers to them, who have worked with Michael, Mary, and the firm through their first, second and third homes, to his loyal and dedicated team, to the esteemed colleagues and collaborators that have helped to articulate the vision. Indeed, it is a fetching, melodic language of home they have spoken over the past two decades.

PAMELA JACCARINO

waterfront

collaborative
on the cape

This classic Cape Cod shingled house on the waterfront looks as if it has been there forever, but it was recently built by architects Shope Reno Wharton with the interior details and furnishings designed by Foley & Cox. The traditional exterior nestles naturally into the landscape, while the interior ushers in a more contemporary aesthetic, with a modern sculptural shell-stone mantel and boldly scaled molding and trim details. The family's art collection influenced the interiors, which act as a backdrop for paintings and sculpture juxtaposed with playful and welcoming furnishings. The intentional combination of the familiar with the inventive and modern resulted in a seaside home with an updated sensibility.

OPPOSITE: Natural shingles, white trim, and blue hydrangea echo the classic elements of the Cape and contrast with the contemporary spirit inside.

OVERLEAF: The great room was designed for ample comfortable seating, with a Basse Terre sofa by Christian Liaigre and woven rattan chairs and ottomans by John Himmel. The floating shelves of black-lacquered steel from KGBL complement a painting by James Nares above the fireplace.

OPPOSITE: The family room is grounded by a striped sisal area rug from Merida and crowned in the center with a cloud chandelier from Apparatus. Natural ramie shades at the windows suit the casual style of the room.

LEFT: A Matthew Fairbanks desk perfectly orients the owners to the water views while working or letter writing.

ABOVE: A flower print by Donald Sultan hangs above a curved console table from Lawson-Fenning.

OVERLEAF: A concrete dining table from Mecox Gardens is surrounded by gray-and-white striped Kirby chairs from the Foley & Cox Collection, with Alex Katz's *Good Afternoon* as the backdrop.

17

ABOVE: Overlooking the inlet, this guest bedroom has a bohemian vibe with Indian print bedding from John Robshaw and geometric prints on pillows. The scattered collection of paper lanterns adds a casual and festive element.

OPPOSITE: A pair of L-shaped teak sectionals transforms the bluestone terrace into an outdoor living room—perfect for lounging and entertaining and offering endless views of the sea and the sailing school in the harbor.

serene

in east hampton

Easy, casual, and carefree was the client directive to Foley & Cox in working on this shingled house in the Hamptons. Originally built in the 1950s, the house required reconsideration and a full reconstruction while staying within the grandfathered footprint. Each material specification, design choice, and furnishings purchase was carefully evaluated to meet the criteria of the project brief. Thoughtful collaboration between the architect, contractor, client, and designer was imperative. The Dutch door opens into a spacious entry, which gives a clue to the result, a mix of low-maintenance practicality with sophisticated furniture, graphic art, and contemporary lighting—a house for today's living. In this sun-filled vacation home, floor-to-ceiling glass walls bring the outdoors in and allow the eye to travel out to the lawn and garden.

OPPOSITE: A Holly Hunt console table and a woven Bolon rug welcome guests to the new home. The Maze table lamp is from Holly Hunt, and the mirror by Mark Albrecht is leather-wrapped steel.

LEFT: The industrial-style stainless-steel and glass wall draws light in and injects a new sensibility to the design.

OPPOSITE: A peaked double-height ceiling and beams create a dramatic effect in the open dining area, which features a Lindsey Adelman light fixture and a painting by Mark Sheinkman.

OVERLEAF: A V-grooved wood-clad ceiling with tie beams amplifies the space in the living room, while the sandy, monochromatic palette unifies the space. The Johnnie Winona Ross painting above the fireplace becomes a focal point when night falls.

ABOVE: In the primary bedroom, tonal off-white textiles combine with reclaimed beams above the windows and a classic Ingo Maurer light fixture to create texture and depth in this tranquil retreat. A Jeri Eisenberg photograph hangs above the bed.

OPPOSITE, TOP: An allée of hornbeam trees lines the edge of the pool in the garden designed by Joseph W. Tyree Landscape Design.

OPPOSITE, BOTTOM: The oval bathtub by Waterworks in the primary bathroom has private garden views. The fixtures are from Dornbracht.

spirited

in southampton

A family compound in Southampton evolved with the construction of this
new beach house for the next generation. We designed the parents' residence
across the street, and with this addition, we were able to create more playful
spaces for children and grandchildren with bright color and a modern
sensibility. A raw red-cedar beamed ceiling and an open stairway with steel
railings create a graphic statement as the "spine" of the home. By carefully
sprinkling antiques and vintage pieces throughout, we were able to infuse a
lived-in patina and a sense of soul into the newly constructed home. With
eight bedrooms and generous open gathering spaces, there is plenty of room
for the next two generations to grow here.

OPPOSITE: Frank Herz's hanging plaster
sculpture *Abstract Cloud #1* is from Flair Home
Collection. The alabaster sphere lamp-on-stand
is Edition Modern.

OVERLEAF: In the open space off the entry,
Foley & Cox shows a deft hand at balancing
vintage, custom, modern, and collected. A
bright-blue stair runner, an entry rug crafted of
recycled rubber, and even the Yves Klein blue
interior of the Ingo Maurer light fixture are at
home with the custom Mondrian-inspired chest
by Richomme.

LEFT: In the main stairwell, a Lindsey Adelman light sculpture of rope-tied glass globes that mimic sea floats creates a focal point and continuity between the three floors. The stair railing evokes a ship rail while the painting by Joseph Richards continues the nautical theme.

OPPOSITE: The brightly geometric pillows and black-and-white artwork by Jack Wells convey the youthful energy of the home, with pattern play and bold graphics.

ABOVE: Liz Roache silkscreened prints are
a color-study focal point in the billiard room,
which is anchored by a bright turquoise
Missoni rug.

OPPOSITE: The living room becomes another
retreat, enlivened by boldly striped carpeting,
colorful paintings by Ethan Boisvert, and
an oversized rattan ceiling fixture from
Atelier Vime.

OVERLEAF: The open kitchen spills onto the
dining patio for easy grilling and indoor/
outdoor living. A glazed fabric from Dedar is
used on the Thomas Hayes counter stools.
Allied Maker pendants add impact.

LEFT: This powder room sings with blues from Holland & Sherry wallcovering. The vanity is a refitted rattan cabinet, and the vintage sconces are from the Paris flea market, adding texture and interest to this small space.

OPPOSITE: The calming colors in the primary bedroom suggest rest and relaxation with a soft blue and white palette. The black-and-white photographs above the bed are by Michael Dweck. The color photograph above the fireplace is *Dawn Patrol* by Katie Holstein.

relaxed

in montauk

Nestled in the trees on a secluded bluff, this house was acquired as a vacation home for a retired executive and his family. With natural shingles and white-painted wood trim, it reflects the vernacular architecture of the east end of Long Island. The interior materials continue this style with a relaxed look of whitewashed wood paneled walls and natural materials, while the furnishings are a mix of clean, contemporary designs and vintage pieces.

The house was designed for indoor/outdoor living, celebrating the ocean views and open plan design for entertaining. On weekends the man of the house holds court in the kitchen. Guests pull up chairs at the island to keep him company while others are having drinks on the deck, the place to be to see the sunsets. Previous collaborations with the clients led to a shorthand in developing a shared design vision, and the results show. "The designers did a great job of understanding us, how we wanted to use our house and our personalities. They hit the nail on the head," says the client.

OPPOSITE: A pair of vintage Danish modern chairs sets the tone in the living room.

OVERLEAF: A light, natural color palette throughout the public spaces creates a cohesive foundation and draws the eye to the dramatic ocean views all around. Sheer linen curtains by Esther Calderon Interiors frame the windows looking out to the ocean. The driftwood coffee table is from Dos Gallos, the sofa from Second Life Interiors, the armchairs from Foley & Cox Home.

OPPOSITE: A bentwood sphere table lamp sits on a glass-and-chrome table from Brueton. The cream linen drapery and charcoal throw pillows are by Dessin Fournir.

ABOVE: The white-oak dining table from Angela Adams and the classic leather Cassina Cab dining chairs seat ten in the space adjacent to the kitchen island and the decks.

OVERLEAF: Purple is one of nature's elegant neutrals; it has a beautiful spectrum of shades to pair with soft shades of sand, seafoam and creams. In the primary bedroom, the geometric rug from La Manufacture Cogolin was inspired by the lavender hues of the sunsets. The Stacked Ball sculpture in the corner is from Tucker Robbins. Private decks with Tulum chairs from the Foley & Cox Outdoor Collection extend the space overlooking the Atlantic.

BELOW: Always in demand, the guest suite is filled with art, books, flowers, and every amenity to make guests feel at home. The bed is from Lawson-Fenning and the sconces are from Urban Archaeology.

OPPOSITE: In the primary bath, an Easton soaking tub is the focal point, sitting beneath *Paperworks* by Gill Wilson. The Foley & Cox Zanzibar bench keeps bath salts, towels, and sponges within reach.

sophisticated

in sag harbor

When it came to designing the interior of his own home, Hamptons architect Frank Greenwald knew who to turn to. We have collaborated with him on many projects, and the ease of communication and compatible aesthetic make our projects successful. Greenwald wanted a modern, but not cold, year-round beach house, and although it is primarily white, it is enhanced with rich, warm Brazilian ipe wood paneling, windows, and doors. We designed the interior, layering on complementary natural materials such as jute and sisal rugs, white linen curtains and shades, and canvas and linen upholstery—the only counterpoint, navy blue in accessories. The palette of blue and white has timeless, universal appeal, especially in common areas where the homeowner and guests alike will find it familiar and welcoming. A few statement pieces and modern classics fit the bill, and all are intentional choices to keep the views of the bay a focal point. As Mary Foley said, "It's a place made for easy living."

OPPOSITE: Paneling fabricated from Brazilian ipe wood brings a richness to the hall, which opens to the main living space. Sailing photographs, shells, and blue hydrangea blossoms evoke summer in Sag Harbor.

OPPOSITE: The grids of windows and central staircase create graphic patterns in the main entry hall. Wall sconces, like portholes, are a nod to sailing and nautical style. The seating niche "captures and contains" jackets, keys, and shoes.

RIGHT: An overscaled mirror reflects the water view. The metal seahorse was a local Hamptons find and whimsically oversees woven barware on the vintage Milo Baughman sideboard.

OPPOSITE AND ABOVE: The expansive living room
is sited for the best views; the seating area includes
a Christian Liaigre sofa, a PK Grasshopper
lounge chair, and a pair of Poul Kjaerholm leather
chairs on a Merida sisal rug. The white Corian
Jane coffee table is from FTF Design Studio.

57

LEFT: The primary bedroom is an ode to blue, with graphic bed linens on the Ovington bed by Foley & Cox and a silkscreen print by James Nares above the bed.

OPPOSITE: The outdoor shower of horizontal ipe wood slats is nestled into the landscape and offers guests the luxury of showering under endless skies.

OVERLEAF: The terrace connects the living and dining space with the pool and the open bay, all furnished with teak furniture and crisp navy-blue canvas umbrellas. The quiet palette and low furnishings allow the spectacular view to remain uninterrupted.

lush
in the bahamas

A tropical paradise is the setting for this Bahamian residence. Its classic white stucco exterior is built in the local genre, but the interiors are filled with light and color, not traditional floral chintz. The clients, a New York City couple with children and grandchildren, wanted a fresh, modern twist on this beach house, a place to display their art, and a respite from Manhattan. As we have collaborated on several projects with them, it was easy to interpret their directive for a low-maintenance, organic, and comfortable environment for this vacation home. After painting the walls a crisp Super White by Benjamin Moore, we infused the interiors with bright color in the art and upholstery so that the views of the turquoise sea and palm trees from all the windows remain focal points.

OPPOSITE AND OVERLEAF: Sheer white linen curtains diffuse the intense sunlight and soften the living room; the floors are covered with woven straw matting rugs. Accents of brilliant blue on Milo Baughman chairs and long lumbar pillows enliven the living room of natural, white, and coral stone.

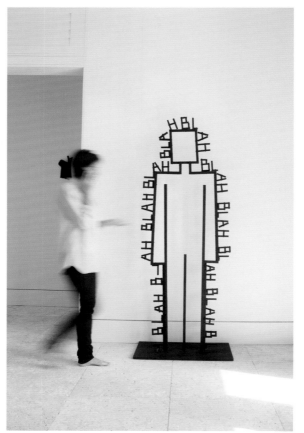

ABOVE, LEFT: A bright chrome-yellow serigraph by
Robert Peterson is the showpiece in the family
room. The sofa is from Lee Industries; the
woven hyacinth-straw ottomans are from Ralph
Lauren Home.

ABOVE, RIGHT: *Mr. Blah, Blah, Blah*, the
whimsical sculpture by Olaf Breuning in the
hallway, reflects the owners' sense of humor.

OPPOSITE: A dining table by Hudson Furniture
and Gio Ponti Superleggera chairs from Cassina
are complemented by *Object with Flaw* by John
Baldessari. The chandelier by Jean-Christophe
Dablemont was discovered at a Paris flea market.

LEFT: A peek into a guest bedroom, with a canopy bed by Lillian August under a ceiling fan by Modern Fan Company.

OPPOSITE: A custom upholstered bed from Bernhardt Industries and a painting by Sandeep Mukherjee create a medley of blues looking out to the sea.

OVERLEAF: At the back of the house, a coral stone terrace shaded by the balcony extends the outdoor living space to the pool with seating by Janus et Cie. The Bahamian climate allows true indoor/outdoor living, and the architecture and interiors were carefully planned to maximize that luxury.

shingled

on the south fork

Initiated as a renovation of a modest 1970s house for a three-generation family, this project evolved into a new build and an opportunity to rethink the design of a summer house on Little Peconic Bay. While the couple had anticipated extensive renovations, they were not expecting a teardown. After the initial shock, they changed gears, and working with architect Joseph Cerami and Foley & Cox, they were able to incorporate their full program and even more. The goal was a comfortable home with all modern amenities, but with a classic shingle style exterior. On the interior, chic and practical are thoughtfully balanced to create a relaxed, welcoming environment for children and guests.

OPPOSITE: A sculptural screen by John Lyle is a dramatic addition to the double-sided fireplace, which also opens to the family room. A Noguchi Akari light fixture and a Hans Wegner Ox chair complete the scene.

OVERLEAF: The expansive living room has views of the bay and opens up to the deck with outdoor seating and dining. Beside the Christian Liaigre sofa is an antique African stool that functions as a side table. The pair of vintage armchairs is from Foley & Cox Home.

LEFT: In the entry, an exuberant red tulip painting hangs above a midcentury console table from Machine Age, updated with newly lacquered drawer fronts.

OPPOSITE: A white Corian coffee table appears to float above the carpet in the living room. A pair of Jean Prouvé Cité chairs from Vitra punctuates the space. The glass sculpture on a travertine pedestal is a 1940s French chemical apparatus from Balsamo Antiques.

OPPOSITE: A brutalist side table from Venfield is used as a night table for the woven-straw bed in the guest room.

ABOVE: The family room seating area features a custom sofa in Janus et Cie indoor-outdoor fabric; the vintage oak chairs are French art deco, designed by André Sornay.

OVERLEAF: In front of the house, the pool area is bordered by trees for privacy and Richard Schultz lounges for comfort while the rear opens directly onto the bay.

transitional

in the hamptons

Creating their first weekend haven was the original objective for this young couple (he grew up in a Foley & Cox–designed home). We oversaw the interior renovation and design, transforming this house into a home for the family of five. Approachable, welcoming, and low maintenance, punctuated by bold, colorful art and eclectic furnishings, the spaces reflect a fresh sensibility to modern living and collecting. But with life transformed during the 2020 global pandemic, this weekend house in East Hampton evolved into the family's permanent home, and it is now the backdrop for the next generation to grow up.

OPPOSITE: A shaded terrace, with upholstered outdoor furniture from RH and a coffee table from Janus et Cie, becomes an outdoor living room with views of the pool and shade garden.

OPPOSITE: A pair of vintage chairs and ottomans found at the Paul Bert market in Paris fit well with a pair of vintage Danish modern chairs from Foley & Cox Home.

BELOW: An upstairs sitting room with rounded-edge furniture and soft upholstery from Verellen is just right for a family with young children.

OVERLEAF: The couple enjoys hosting parties for friends and their extended family in the spacious dining room. The table and chairs are from STUDIOTWENTYSEVEN and the chandelier from French artist Ann-Pierre Malval. The painting is by Sebastian Black.

BELOW: The primary bedroom has a comfortable seating area. The pendant light fixture is from Pinch in London, and the linen area rug from Aronson's. The loveseat and custom bed are Foley & Cox Home. A photograph by Peter Margonelli hangs over the bed.

OPPOSITE: In the primary bathroom, a Mariette Himes Gomez chair upholstered in terry cloth is the perfect perch at bath time.

OPPOSITE: Bright fabrics, bold art, and colorful accessories energize the children's playroom. A denim sofa from Design Within Reach anchors the room with red bean bag chairs from Room & Board.

RIGHT: A soft pastel lavender palette on walls and textiles create a soothing environment for the daughter's room. Above the bed are baby animals photographed by Sharon Montrose.

cityscapes

curated

in the city

One of the firm's first clients, this couple has collaborated with us for the past twenty years as their lives evolved in the city and in the country, with children growing up and now on their own. This apartment was designed for their "empty nest" period, and the couple enjoyed working with the design team to devise solutions for the amenities the apartment lacked. A floating wall, imagined by us and constructed and installed by Scordio Construction, was placed in the living room to hang major works of art.

White walls throughout provide a backdrop for a rotation of art from their collection. The clients love the cozy multi-functional den, the cushy carpet in the bedroom. In this apartment across from Madison Square Park, orientation toward the view was important and considered. For this investment executive and board president of a major New York City art institution, entertaining for family, friends, and business colleagues is an important aspect of their home life. The space is just right for them, and they speak a design shorthand with us, resulting in a space that looks beautiful and functions perfectly, while reflecting their own personal style—comfortable and chic.

OPPOSITE: *Stranger in the Village #11* by Glenn Ligon hangs on the floating wall in the living room. The cocktail table is by Jacques Adnet and coal side table by Jim Zivic.

LEFT: A gallery-like atmosphere throughout the apartment showcases the clients' collections—glimpsed here are works by John Chamberlain and Donald Judd.

OPPOSITE: The sectional in pressed linen by Maharam and the canyon-brown leather-and-chrome ottoman are both custom by De Angelis. The Hans Wegner Papa Bear chair from Wyeth has exposed teak arms and original wool upholstery.

OVERLEAF: The living room furnishings are arranged for the best views of Madison Square Park. The curved sofa was custom made by De Angelis. The modular T22C elmwood coffee table, designed by Pierre Chapo about 1970, is from the Magen H. Gallery. A pair of Clam chairs were designed by Philip Arctander from Almond & Co.

LEFT: The carpet in the primary bedroom is from Tai Ping Carpet and the cabinet is custom by KGBL.

OPPOSITE: John Baldessari's print *Noses & Ears Etc: Torso and Head (With Nose and Ear)* hangs over the banquette in the dining alcove. The recessed grid of lights in the kitchen was part of the overall lighting plan developed by Bill Schwinghammer.

OPPOSITE: A rosewood Waterfall desk from Twentieth LA sits in front of a wall of horizontal unit shelving by Design Freres. The Bird desk chair in cognac leather is by Preben Fabricus from Almond & Co.

RIGHT: A French midcentury sideboard from Foley & Cox Home was retrofitted as a sink with a black absolute honed marble-top; the Rougier Tulip lamp is from Little Paris Antiques.

modern

in manhattan

Architect Douglas Wright, Donadic Construction, and Foley & Cox
collaborated on a renovation of this "classic six" Park Avenue apartment to
maximize square footage and create public and private spaces for a finance
executive and his young family. The goal was sophisticated urban living
balanced with modern amenities for comfort and ease. Respecting the
traditional roots of the architecture, the designers were able to reconfigure the
spaces and create functionality for today. Shades of eggshell and warm whites
create the backdrop in this light-filled space for color and texture layered on in
the textiles and art. Gone are the heavy moldings and trappings of a stuffy past.
As Michael Cox said: "The space is respectful of its classic Park Avenue location
and prewar traditions, but it is updated to reflect a new generation."

OPPOSITE: The Anigre wood–paneled library
and office has an expansive view, magnified by
the mirrored reflection in the window jamb.
The cabinet doors are fitted with leather and
brass pulls. A warm suede floor covering from
Keleen Leathers creates a soft foundation this
stylish space.

LEFT: Blue upholstered corner chairs custom made by Richomme welcome guests in the entryway. Wide stripes of gray and white marble draw the eye in. The trellis ceiling light fixture is from Modulighter.

OPPOSITE: The crushed-bamboo dining table is by Wyeth. Above is a Cloud chandelier from Apparatus. White trapunto-detailed cashmere sheers frame the windows.

OVERLEAF: A Giacometti-inspired table by Silas Seandel and a nickel chain-link light by Hudson Furniture are finishing touches in this gracious living room, with exclamations of color in paintings, pillows, and orchids.

OPPOSITE: The banquette designed with a bold chocolate and lavender woven leather and table from Soane Britain make a perfect setting for a casual breakfast or a romantic dinner.

RIGHT: The primary bedroom features the Foley & Cox Collection Ovington bed, a parchment bedside table by Roman Thomas, and a plaster chandelier from the Thomas Gallery.

LEFT: The children's rooms are infused with primary colors in the carpets and upholstery.

OPPOSITE: Curtains are a crisp bright blue-and-white geometric patterned fabric by Victoria Hagan. A playful Birdie's Nest light from Ingo Maurer adds a touch of whimsy on the ceiling.

tranquil
in boston

High above the city in the Mandarin Oriental Hotel, we created a calm oasis for an active young family. The client had seen an article she loved on our firm in a magazine, ripped it out, and carried it around in her handbag for two years. When the couple found this apartment, she knew just who to call. Working with F. H. Perry, we renovated the space and introduced a monochromatic palette with natural colors in the furnishings and materials. Custom furniture was designed for the space, with soft linen sheers for the windows and artwork with nature and landscape themes softening the modern aesthetic. By consistently maintaining a neutral palette and focusing on texture rather than pattern, we were able to create a soothing sanctuary in the heart of the city.

OPPOSITE: A still life of white textured vases and amaryllis on a woven leather console from Bottega Veneta in the hall welcomes the family to their new home.

OVERLEAF: A mushroom and oatmeal color palette in the living room, rendered in materials like suede and cashmere, softens the space. The ebony crushed-bamboo coffee table from Wyeth and the sumptuous chairs from Christian Liaigre sit on a tonal carpet. Two images from the Branch series by Don Freeman balance the room.

OPPOSITE: A bench upholstered in linen from Christian Liaigre for Holly Hunt welcomes guests in the entry. The painting above is by Johnnie Winona Ross; the woven suede floor covering is from Keleen Leathers.

RIGHT: The dining area features a painting of sky and clouds by Kathryn Lynch and a pedestal table by Holly Hunt with custom De Angelis–upholstered chairs.

LEFT: The children's bedroom is layered with sophisticated elements such as a Dodu cream felt upholstered bed from Blu Dot and hand-sewn carpet from Elizabeth Eakins.

OPPOSITE: The primary bedroom continues the study of layered neutrals with cashmere, parchment, and ceramics all colored in creams. The night tables are by Roman Thomas; the ethereal image of trees is by photographer Jeri Eisenberg. A Claudia Barberi hand-knit cashmere throw lies at the foot of the bed.

eloquent
on the park

A prestigious Central Park West address in a Robert A. M. Stern Architects–
designed luxury tower is the setting of a "home away from home" for
a Canadian television and film producer couple. Sophisticated classic
architectural detailing throughout the interior contrasts with modern
furnishings and contemporary art on the walls. A tonal, monochromatic
approach to the rooms maximizes the sense of spaciousness and keeps
the focus on the breathtaking view of the Manhattan skyline.

Reflecting on their experience with the firm, the clients commented, "Foley &
Cox have left an indelible imprint on our lives and in our home. They seek to
find the most personal of detail in every consideration and opportunity they
choose for their clients. The greatest compliment we can pay the designers and
their extraordinary team is that not a day goes by when we don't think about
or reflect on their exquisite taste and design acumen."

OPPOSITE: A view into the living space shows the
open plan seating and dining areas.

OVERLEAF: An overscaled painting by Lloyd
Martin hangs over the sofa, which is flanked by
Roman Thomas chairs. The hand-blown
sconces are by glass artist Alison Berger.

LEFT: A custom armchair upholstered in butter soft suede provides a comfortable seat in the primary bedroom.

OPPOSITE: A classical pilaster and paneling in warm cream add beautiful detailing to a seating area with a custom sofa from Foley & Cox Home.

OPPOSITE: A wrought-metal base table with a glass top by Silas Seandel holds pride of place in the dining room. Henry Dean hurricanes in "smoke" add moody texture to the tablescape.

old world
in europe

In six classic limestone townhouses called Noble Row, the Foley & Cox design team brought a sophisticated, glamorous interpretation to the old-world-style interiors. Designed by Gregory Tuck Architecture, the houses reflect a rich architectural tradition with meticulously executed details in the finest Beaux-Arts style. In the entrance halls, a grand staircase with lyrical wrought-iron railings sets the tone for these elegant homes. A large crystal chandelier glistens against the limestone floors, columns, and walls, all in a soft cream color palette. The real estate developer was looking for a signature Ralph Lauren style, and Foley & Cox was the perfect partner to realize this project. Hallmarks of the nineteenth century with its timeless elegance and exacting craftsmanship were designed and brought to life for twenty-first-century living. Incorporating every luxurious detail and every modern amenity, these residences were designed to be delivered "turn-key" so the new owner could arrive with a toothbrush and immediately begin living and entertaining. Kitchens were stocked, beds fully dressed, dining tables set for a dinner party—every selection was thoughtfully considered for a comprehensive and elegant environment.

OPPOSITE: A dramatic double-height entry in limestone with decorative iron railings sets the tone for the project.

LEFT: An intricately carved marble chimney piece by Chesney is in contrasted with the clean lines of a polished nickel mirror that reflects the cut-crystal chandelier.

OPPOSITE: A gallery wall of eclectic photographs, line drawings, and watercolors is unified by the black and silver-leaf finishing details provided by Skyframe. The formality of the room is softened by the natural wool sisal rug.

OVERLEAF: A scheme of crisp black and white with brass accents defines the Christopher Peacock kitchen, which is a luxurious setting not just for cooking but also for entertaining. Black leather stools pulled up at the island, paneling details, and white milk-glass pendant lighting make the space feel like a private club.

OPPOSITE AND RIGHT: Simply framed artwork, a fanciful chandelier, black-and-white flower embroidered draperies, and a baroque gilded mirror above the white marble Chesney fireplace mantel are the finishing touches in this romantic bedroom. Feminine florals and sharp black-and-white stripes balance the yin and yang of this primary suite.

eclectic
on the hudson

Designed with views of the Hudson River, the Statue of Liberty, and the Manhattan skyline as the backdrop, these three suites at the Liberty National Golf Club were created primarily for the owners and members to use while enjoying the club. Foley & Cox was invited to transform the existing hotel-like rooms into more comfortable spaces with a residential feel. Since the suites are available for member bookings, practical considerations of durable surfaces, performance fabrics, and sustainable materials were incorporated into the design program. Expansive windows and modern, relaxed furnishings set the tone of the open plan spaces, with layers of textiles to soften the slick surfaces and glass walls and windows. Incorporating color and texture with curated art, books, and accessories transformed the minimalist look. Design director Zuni Madera commented that being in the rooms feels like floating on a ship.

OPPOSITE: Books and artwork help make this a "home away from home." Dramatic views of the Manhattan skyline are framed by windows with concealed shades from Rosehyll Studio.

OVERLEAF: The open plan living and dining spaces are furnished with a soft palette of creams, grays, and blues inspired by the sky and water views. A Sean Lavin light fixture hangs above the game table with Foley & Cox Collection chairs upholstered in Ultrasuede.

LEFT: A bold black-and-white striped wall creates a transition from the entry to the living room in this villa with its dark wood floors and black-and-white artwork. The light fixture is an Emerson chandelier by Arteriors.

OPPOSITE: Open shelving for books and art conveys a sense of welcome and comfort; a translucent paper Noguchi lamp adds a functional sculptural element.

OVERLEAF: Awakening guests are greeted by uninterrupted views of the Hudson River and the Statue of Liberty. The painting above the bed was commissioned from London-based artist Jan Erika. The leather-wrapped brass light fixture is from Ralph Lauren Home.

creative
in new york

A staid prewar apartment with small rooms and dim light challenged Foley &
Cox to create a new environment for a vibrant couple in the design and beauty
industries. She'd been inspired by the "brass and sass" sets of the TV show
"Empire;" he had been Michael Cox's boss and mentor at Ralph Lauren. Layer
in years of friendship, many other design collaborations, and a new goal:
updating a traditional apartment and making it relevant for today with clean,
modern lines and a dose of modern art. Mix in consideration of the comfort
of their beloved dog, Annie.

The project was accomplished in partnership with architect Eric Gartner of
SPG Architects, who, over the course of two years, gutted the interior, removed
all the restrictive built-in millwork, and changed the vibe of the space with
steel and glass walls, graphic white beams, simply framed windows. Foley & Cox
brought in luxury and light with contemporary clean-lined upholstery and
furniture, filled the walls with colorful artwork, and injected a modern attitude.

OPPOSITE: A dramatic photograph, *Virtue,
Bode-Museum, Berlin* by Reinhard Görner,
sets the scene in the hallway. A classic paper
lamp by Ingo Maurer rests on the side table by
Reagan Hayes.

OVERLEAF: A custom eight-foot-long sofa fills
the living room and grounds the large colorful
paintings by Ethan Boisvert above. A pair of
favorite Ralph Lauren chairs and glass-topped
coffee tables are a nod to earlier collaborations.
The leather bench is from James Devlin and
the side tables are from The Future Perfect.

147

OPPOSITE: A glimpse of the home office through steel-and-glass walls, with a lounge chair by Studio Van den Akker; a pair of Eames chairs flank a desk by Richard Wrightman.

BELOW: A sensitively inserted glass wall creates a seamless transition from the "entertaining" living room to the "movie-watching" family room. The custom coffee table is by Silas Seandel. The bold block prints are by Liz Roache.

OPPOSITE: The simple shade on the window frames a view of the Hudson River from the primary bedroom. Over the bed is an abstract painting by Sabine Maes.

RIGHT AND BELOW: Gold accents in lighting, wallcovering, drawer fronts, and even gilded leaves add glamour to the primary suite. The bedside tables are from Egg Collective and the Martine bed is from the Foley & Cox Collection.

classic

on park avenue

After completing a home in the Hamptons for these clients, we were asked to refresh their newly acquired prewar apartment on the Upper East Side. The couple wanted to keep the elegant crown moldings and beautiful herringbone floors, but they needed new amenities including an updated kitchen, walk-in closets, and a wet bar for entertaining. The guest room needed to do double duty as a part-time nursery for visits from their new grandchild. As inveterate travelers and owners of a major travel agency, they wanted their home to reflect an international style and incorporate pieces they had admired and collected on their trips around the world. Foley & Cox collaborated with architect Douglas Wright on the renovation to maintain the original charm of the apartment but imbue it with a sense of the clients' style and layer in luxurious materials and artwork. The result perfectly reflects our appreciation of prewar architectural details balanced with our passion for innovative designs, modern amenities, and artisan-made furnishings.

OPPOSITE: A corner of the living room was designed for an intimate dinner or an occasional workspace. The banquette by Peruvian Touch and the tea table from Richomme were custom made for perfect, multi-functional scale. On the wall is a Dai Ban sculpture from Carrie Haddad Gallery.

OVERLEAF: The living room seating features a custom sofa and upholstered armchairs atop a luxe area rug from Fort Street Studio. The cocktail table is from Silas Seandel Studio, the floor lamp from The Future Perfect. A painting by Lloyd Martin hangs opposite the mirrored overmantel.

OPPOSITE: The traditional Park Avenue kitchen feels freshly reinterpreted in navy and white, with a built-in banquette with storage and a Saarinen Tulip table. An Urban Electric pendant hangs above.

RIGHT: The foyer has a spacious and luxurious feel with a pedestal table from Foley & Cox Home and a "Facets" brass chandelier from Innermost. The original herringbone floors mix perfectly with contemporary furnishings.

OPPOSITE AND ABOVE: The walls of the library/
den are papered in Holland & Sherry with blue
painted windows and door trim. The cocktail
table from The Future Perfect is a Foley & Cox
favorite. The Oxford desk chair, designed by
Arne Jacobsen from Fritz Hansen, creates an
executive home office in front of the windows.

OVERLEAF: The clients found the pendant light
on a trip to Marrakech. The bed is the Foley &
Cox Martine, table lamps are from Aubèry, Inc.,
and the chaise longue was fabricated by Peruvian
Touch in Holly Hunt fabric.

countryside

majestic
in the mountains

High on a mountaintop outside of Kitzbühel, Austria, we created the alpine lodge of our clients' dreams. As part of the process, we researched regional history, Black Forest style, and Tyrolean design traditions. We visited the area at different seasons, seeing it in winter, when it looks like a snowy fairy-tale setting, and during spring, when wildflowers and the famous edelweiss are in bloom.

The client, who appreciates design that improves with age and use, has enjoyed this retreat for more than twenty years, a testament to the timeless approach of Foley & Cox. We commissioned local furniture makers and artisans to design custom pieces, haunted local antique shops for accessories, and supplemented them with pieces from New York showrooms and Paris flea markets. Linens were sourced from Salzburg, cushions were fabricated in the loden cloth of traditional jackets, and antique beer steins were displayed on a vivid red cloth-wrapped entry console. Upon entering the house and experiencing the mountain views, visitors sometimes wish that they will be snowbound, an excuse to remain in the magical retreat.

OPPOSITE: An open dining and lounging terrace takes advantage of the sweeping mountain views, furnished with sturdy, rustic furniture that endures winter weather conditions.

OVERLEAF: The great room is constructed of massive wood beams that impart character and frame the window views. The cocktail tables are overscaled as are the globe lanterns from Jamb in London. The window seats are upholstered in plaid woven leather from Lance Wovens with pillows and throws from Frauenschuh.

OPPOSITE: The white stucco fireplace takes pride of place in the sitting room. A cowhide rug, Black Forest carving, and shearling pillows imbue the space with authenticity and a sense of place.

RIGHT: In the primary bedroom, the fireplace and seating area are enhanced by a large antler chandelier from Linda Horn. The daybed is custom made of winter-white cashmere and shearling by De Angelis.

LEFT: Guests are welcomed by traditional elements of horn and pewter displayed on a modern Parsons console, upholstered in local red loden.

OPPOSITE: Family breakfasts are brightened with red and yellow—a warm retreat during the "white out" of winter.

OVERLEAF: A circular Jacuzzi, fundamental to Austrian health and well-being, is the heart of the wellness center of the chalet. Naturally sited boulders anchor the space to its mountainside setting.

ABOVE: Deerskin, loden, wool, and cashmere warm the stucco walls and rustic beams of this guest suite. Cowbells can be heard from neighboring farms.

OPPOSITE: Thoughtfully integrated into the landscape, the house nestles into the mountainside.

contemporary

in brookline

In this contemporary house outside of Boston, designed by architects Shope Reno Wharton, we created interiors as a backdrop to the art collection. A former Fortune 500 executive and his wife were ready for downsizing to a smaller home with an updated aesthetic, bespoke detailing, and a streamlined environment. Millwork details recede rather than project, drapes soften windows with tonal hand embroidery, and soft, neutral colors harmoniously form the foundation. The modern architectural elements provide a clean canvas for their furnishings and collection of paintings and sculpture. The end result: a vibrant home that reflects a new chapter for the clients.

OPPOSITE: A wall of neon-colored Marilyn Monroe portraits by Andy Warhol creates a dramatic entry, with a view into the living room. The black-and-white calligraphic rug is from Doris Leslie Blau.

OPPOSITE: The cantilevered stair of oak, steel, and glass is sculptural itself, a natural setting for the owners' art collection. The leather handrail is by Lance Wovens and the bench from Dennis Miller; the light fixture is by Cameron House Design.

ABOVE, LEFT: A glazed linen-wrapped Christian Liaigre coffee table centers the living room.

ABOVE, RIGHT: In the hallway, a grid of geometric art by Donald Judd repeats the architectural pattern of the black casement windows. Ceiling fixtures are by Urban Electric.

OVERLEAF: The architects agree that "we like the idea of the home as a place of refuge but also as a gallery where the owners can display and enjoy artwork and sculptures that they collect." The sofas are custom from McLaughlin Upholstery, the cocktail table is by Christian Liaigre, side table by Hudson Furniture. The dining table is by Cliff Young with chairs from Holly Hunt. A Fernand Léger lithograph hangs above a custom console by John Lyle, while a white marble sculpture by Hans Arp is mounted on an ebonized pedestal. Light fixtures are by Studio Van den Akker.

OPPOSITE: In the upstairs sitting room, the gracefully arched ceiling softens the geometry of the cerused oak millwork. The Paris lounge chairs by Foley & Cox and custom ottoman are upholstered in embossed leather from Moore and Giles. The custom rug is from Merida and the ceiling fixture is from John Rosselli & Associates.

RIGHT: Umber-stained white-oak paneling covers the walls of the library, and a grid motif repeats in the Tibetano carpet. A Cenotaph lamp from The Future Perfect sits beside the custom-tailored sofa from McLaughlin Upholstery Company.

LEFT: The breakfast room is brightened with a Milton Avery painting above the console. The Carmel dining table is by Ferrell Mittman; the chairs are custom made by Peruvian Touch. The tole shade ceiling fixture is from Charles Edwards.

OPPOSITE: Light fixtures by Roll & Hill and Thomas Hayes counter stools transform this classic white kitchen into the chic heart of the house.

ABOVE: The primary bedroom is a sanctuary infused with quiet touches of lavender, a favorite shade of the homeowner. Hand-sewn drapery by Fine Lines frames the garden view. A suite of Matisse lithographs hangs above a custom bed from McLaughlin Upholstery Company. The light fixture is from The Future Perfect, the chaise longue is from Holly Hunt, and the floor lamp is by Christian Liaigre.

OPPOSITE: A guest bathroom is a study in understatement with a custom vanity of stained oak and a vanilla-cream marble baseboard installed flush with the walls. A black Vola faucet is an unexpected accent. The mirror is in black forged iron from Soane Britain; the Voyager brass wall sconces are by Allied Maker.

traditional
in connecticut

With two children off to college and the family dynamic shifting, the clients
were ready for a lifestyle change. A collaboration between Austin Patterson
Disston Architects and Foley & Cox and a riverside lot in Connecticut were
the basis for this newly constructed home. We were able to repurpose
and revitalize family heirlooms, a priority for the clients. Our goal to create
a relaxed, comfortable family house was achieved with a mix of family
furnishings, antiques, new art, and custom upholstery. Unexpected, brilliant
color in the pantry and powder room—bright blues and oranges—make these
traditional spaces a counterpoint to the soft, comforting palette throughout
the rest of the house. A seamless integration of the familiar and new make this
new home feel as if it has already been loved by many generations.

OPPOSITE: A Saarinen Tulip table circled by
woven rattan dining chairs and matchstick
window shades are a natural in the breakfast
alcove with river views.

OPPOSITE: Traditional white-oak paneled walls and a coffered ceiling are energized with the addition of a modern ceiling light fixture by Apparatus and the classic desk chair from Foley & Cox Home. A limestone bolection mantel from Chesney with herringbone brick firebox is the transitional element in the room.

RIGHT: View from the library through the center hallway with its paneling and column detailing to the living room fireplace.

LEFT: The wallpaper, Frontier Gondola from Cole & Sons, is the star of this powder room. The marble-topped vanity is custom made. Sconces from Urban Electric flank a vintage mirror painted orange to mimic the lanterns of the gondolas.

OPPOSITE: A fireplace from Chesney establishes the center line of the living room. A blend of modern and traditional upholstery surrounds the brutalist bronze cocktail table. Timeless light fixtures from Charles Edwards are reflected in the mirror, which is painted the same color as the walls to blend into the millwork.

OVERLEAF: Comfort is the key to the family room with a traditional fireplace, a modern frame television mounted above, and soft upholstery to make the room welcoming. Extra depth was built into the sectional to enhance the seat and make movie watching cozy. A balanced mix of patterns, stripes, and florals evoke the classicism of Connecticut.

bespoke
in austria

A young Austrian couple, he the nephew of a longtime client, wanted an integrated palette for their dream home at the base of the Kaiser Mountains in Austria. After searching for more than five years, they finally found the perfect site in a lush valley to construct their ideal family home and working farm. The location informed the interior architecture, color, and materials, becoming the foundation for their growing family's life. Rustic details combine with modern elements for a fresh take on the traditional alpine lifestyle. Expansive windows and open spaces maximize the panoramic views. Bold modern lighting, custom furniture, and pieces from local Austrian artisans mix seamlessly with a palette rooted in nature.

OPPOSITE: The primary suite has a breathtaking view of the mountains. The Forsyth shearling chair by the window sits on a Holland & Sherry rug.

OPPOSITE AND OVERLEAF: The barrel-vaulted
ceiling in reclaimed brick between salvaged
beams sets the stage for layers of natural
materials from linen to cashmere, leather to
shearling. The colors of nature flowing through
windows are reflected in a loden, moss, cork,
and walnut color palette. The seating area is
anchored by, floor covering from Merida, a
coffee table from FAIR, Lief wood-and-leather
chairs, and lighting from Apparatus.

OPPOSITE: A sculptural light fixture from Luke Lamp Co. hangs above the kitchen island, a counterpoint to the antiques on the window ledge. The leather counter stools are from BDDW.

LEFT: A swooping, custom hand-wrought iron handrail complements the natural, unstained oak stairway.

BELOW: The dining room floor is an overscaled herringbone pattern. Black leather Cab dining chairs from Cassina surround a table hand made by a local artisan; the pendant lighting is Bocci from DDC. The Circle in Square mirror is from Brenda Antin Antiques.

stunning
in scarsdale

Honoring the classic Tudor-style architecture of this house was the inspiration for this renovation in Scarsdale, New York. The owners (she the daughter of Foley & Cox clients) wanted to balance the history of the house with modern amenities for their young, growing family. A close collaboration with architect Rosamund Young established a respectful balance of old and new. The proportions of rooms were retained, and floors and moldings were sensitively restored by the Cum Laude Group. We enlivened the interiors with a dramatic forest-green scheme in the living room, a mural-papered dining room, and boldly veined marble sprinkled throughout. The saturated palette transformed the living room. The dark stained floors and wood-framed furniture complete the deep tonal look, respecting the original architecture, while Fornasetti cloud wallcovering on the ceiling infuses new life into the room.

OPPOSITE: A chocolate sisal rug creates circulation in the center entry hall, which opens to the dining room with its scenic wallpaper by Calico. The chandelier is made of painted rope by Bone Simple Design, and the dining chairs are from Foley & Cox Home.

OVERLEAF: The custom Arabescato Corchia fireplace mantel from Bas Stone and photograph by Bill Armstrong are the focal point of the living room. The rich wall color is Studio Green by Farrow and Ball. The walnut cocktail table is by DeMuro Das; the wool sisal rug is by Merida. Sconces by Articolo flank the photograph.

LEFT: The family room is energized by a wall sculpture by Anthony Liggins. A soft plush rug and comfortable seating practically upholstered in performance fabric make watching movies with the family a relaxed pleasure.

OPPOSITE: A game table creates an inviting zone within the living room that sometimes multitasks as a quiet work space.

LEFT: A wall sculpture by Dai Ban from the Carrie Haddad Gallery hangs above the dining room fireplace. The boldly veined marble of the fireplace surround is a thread of design continuity between living, dining, and kitchen.

OPPOSITE: A Saarinen dining table and black leather Cab chairs from Design Within Reach create a casual breakfast area in the kitchen. A pendant lamp by Bhon Bhon and a pair of milk-glass and nickel-trim globes over the island play nicely together on the open ceiling plane of the kitchen and breakfast spaces.

OPPOSITE: A soft shade of blue washes the walls of the primary bedroom. The window treatment fabric is by Christopher Farr; the alabaster wall sconces are from Allied Maker.

RIGHT: The whimsical wallpaper in the children's room is Studio Four NYC with a custom turquoise ceiling light fixture by Avantgarden through 1stDibs.

refined

in greenwich

Creating a new primary residence for a fashion executive and his wife was
not a challenge for us since it was our fifth project together. The clients were
beginning a new chapter of their lives and wanted a modern design aesthetic
while avoiding cold minimalism. This was achieved, even in the midst of a
global pandemic, by integrating some of the furniture the couple already owned
and using a warm color palette and textures throughout.

The exterior is a classic Connecticut stone house, designed by Cormac Byrne
and built by Joe Nannariello. The interior is washed in shades of fresh white
paint, creating a backdrop for comfortable upholstery, soft woven rugs, and the
clients' collections. An outdoor living room and fireplace is a favorite place to
relax and entertain friends and family surrounded by beautiful gardens designed
by Renée Byers.

OPPOSITE: Four chocolate brown armchairs,
rather than an expected sofa, circle the pair of
round glass cocktail tables by Desiron.

OPPOSITE: The family room features a wood-beamed coffered ceiling inset with Philip Jeffries grasscloth and a pair of paintings by Ethan Boisvert above woven rattan consoles by Ralph Lauren Home. The Artistic Frame armchairs, upholstered in Holland & Sherry fabric, soften an overscaled steel-and-glass cocktail table. The ceiling grid pattern intentionally repeats in the pattern of the floor covering.

LEFT: Floor-to-ceiling shelving in natural stained white oak showcases the owner's collection and can be accessed using a contemporary library ladder.

OPPOSITE: To create a timeless kitchen, classic subway tiles are grouted with gray and white cabinets are centered by gray counters and floors. The base of the center island is ebony-stained for bold contrast and anchors the room.

RIGHT: The formal dining room, with upholstered dining chairs from Artistic Frame, has a round pedestal table custom made by Richomme that expands to seat twelve. The modern chandelier is from Ralph Lauren Home. Above the fireplace is *Wide Oak* by David Konigsberg.

ABOVE, LEFT: The primary bathroom is spacious enough for two custom vanities with an oval soaking tub in between. The pendant light fixture is from Ralph Lauren Home.

ABOVE, RIGHT: A deep gray marble sink in the powder room has a pair of streamlined black pendant lights flanking a round art deco mirror.

OPPOSITE: The guest room has a Noguchi light fixture and an upholstered bed from Serena & Lily with bedside lamps from Ralph Lauren Home. A group of Asian prints above the bed brings in layers of pattern and cultural interest.

OVERLEAF: Connecticut bluestone walls, the epitome of garden living, are the backdrop for the outdoor living room, made cozy with a woven rug from Annie Selke. The overscaled cocktail table accommodates drinks and casual meals in front of the fire. The teak swivel chairs are by Gloster Furniture; woven chairs are from Brown Jordan. The wall lantern is from Troy Lighting.

streamlined

in the air

Space and aviation safety considerations made designing the interior of this private plane a challenge. But sumptuous materials in upholstery, carpeting, and accessories created a luxe environment for the client, a retired Formula 1 race car driver. Inspiration from the client came in the form of a Lanvin silver leather sneaker and led the way to layers of perforated leathers, the finest cashmere, men's suiting quality wools, and touches of sterling silver, all in a streamlined color palette of chocolate, black, cream, and silver. Incorporating comfortable seating and refined dining as well as a galley kitchen and small bathroom was all accomplished working with the Bombadier team in Canada. Having worked with the client before on multiple residences, we were able to interpret his direction, leading his guest passengers to describe this as the most beautiful and luxurious aircraft they had ever experienced.

OPPOSITE: The galley kitchen in a black matte lacquered finish is seamless and understated with all the necessary amenities concealed within curved cabinetry.

LEFT: Light-filled off-white Ultrasuede walls and ceiling balance the hand-woven carpeting and silver leather seats.

OPPOSITE: Lush, cushioned seats are softened further with cashmere throws and crocodile leather pillows. Details like the Baccarat crystal vase of calla lilies and modern crystal lamp next to the sofa are elegant touches evocative of residential interiors.

OVERLEAF: The table is set for afternoon tea with crisp white linens, Wedgwood china, Puiforcat silver, and a Frank Gehry–designed vase of white flowers.

luxurious
on a yacht

Designing the interior of a luxe yacht was not a daunting prospect for Foley & Cox, as we had already worked with this client on multiple residential projects in Europe. We transformed the 150-foot vessel into a home on the sea with all the luxury appointments: custom plush upholstered furniture from De Angelis mixed with elegant accessories and artisan details throughout, bringing a sophisticated and streamlined aesthetic to the interiors. We worked quickly and efficiently with the master boatyard Composite Works in La Ciotat, France, and collaborated directly with the client on all selections so the boat could be ready as a summer surprise for his family. A dedicated shopping trip to the markets in Clignancourt in Paris netted several of the antique and vintage treasures that add patina and soul and bring the elegance of luxurious residential interiors to this floating paradise. The re-fit of this boat won best of the year in an international yacht design competition.

OPPOSITE: A custom glass-topped dining table, with BDV Decoration dining chairs, is set with dinnerware from Muriel Grateau in Paris, silverware from Puiforcat, and Riedel crystal. The dining space is open to the main salon with views of the embarkment deck.

BELOW: Extra-long white sofas from De Angelis are upholstered in Rogers & Goffigon linen and provide comfortable seating in the main salon. A custom crushed-bamboo coffee table is by Paul Ebbits; the abaca floor covering is by Jeremy Dylan in New York. Books, accessories, artwork, and orchids convey the warmth of home the client desired.

OPPOSITE: A private office/sitting room off the primary suite features a desk by Mark Albrecht and custom De Angelis sofa covered in Manuel Canovas white canvas. A painting by James Welling hangs on walls upholstered in padded leather squares by Keleen Leathers.

OPPOSITE: Horizontal bands of polished mahogany and white lacquer expand the headboard of the primary cabin. The bedside chests were custom made by Richomme; the Lucite lamps are from Alan Moss. The custom bed is finished with the Vienna collection bedding by Olatz.

ABOVE: More than 150 feet of streamlined, floating luxury, this vessel traverses the Mediterranean while keeping the owners perfectly relaxed.

OVERLEAF: Guests are greeted by a pair of teak chaises upholstered in white canvas. The round black end tables are from the Mia collection at Holly Hunt. The directors' chairs at the long table are bamboo and leather from McGuire Furniture. The banquette in the stern is upholstered in black canvas with countless pillows for comfortable seating and sunbathing.

VINCENT VAN GOGH
The Lost Arles Sketchbook

WELSH-OVCHAROV

WALTON FORD

project credits

COLLABORATIVE ON THE CAPE
Architect: Shope Reno Wharton
Builder: Thoughtforms
Photographer: Peter Margonelli

SERENE IN EAST HAMPTON
Architect: Studio Pedrazzi Architects
Builder: N. Zappola & Associates
Landscape Architect: Joseph W. Tyree Landscape Design, Inc.
Photographer: Peter Margonelli

SPIRITED IN SOUTHAMPTON
Architect: Joseph Cerami Architects
Builder: BK Kuck Construction
Landscape Architect: Joseph W. Tyree Landscape Design, Inc.
Photographer: Tim Lenz

RELAXED IN MONTAUK
Photographer: Peter Margonelli

SOPHISTICATED IN SAG HARBOR
Architect: Frank Greenwald
Photographer: Bruce Buck

LUSH IN THE BAHAMAS
Architect: Vitalini Corazzini Architects
Architect: AB Architects
Photographer: Brantley Photo

SHINGLED ON THE SOUTH FORK
Architect: Joseph Cerami Architects
Builder: BK Kuck Construction
Landscape Architect: Joseph W. Tyree Landscape Design, Inc.
Photographer: Mark Roskams

TRANSITIONAL IN THE HAMPTONS
Builder: N. Zappola & Associates
Photographer: Peter Margonelli

CURATED IN THE CITY
Architect: SPG Architects
Lighting Designer: Schwinghammer Lighting
Builder: Scordio Construction
Photographer: Bjorn Wallander

MODERN IN MANHATTAN
Architect: Douglas C. Wright Architects
Builder: S. Donadic Inc.
Photographer: Bjorn Wallander

TRANQUIL IN BOSTON
Builder: F.H. Perry
Photographer: Bjorn Wallander

ELOQUENT ON THE PARK
Photographer: David Gilbert

OLD WORLD IN EUROPE
Architect: Gregory Tuck Architecture
Developer: Konstantin Akimov, A Project Development, LLC
Builder: Smart Pro Consulting Inc.
Photographer: Bjorn Wallander

ECLECTIC ON THE HUDSON
Photographer: Tim Lenz

CREATIVE IN NEW YORK
Architect: SPG Architects
Builder: A-Plus Interior Remodeling
Photographer: Peter Margonelli

CLASSIC ON PARK AVENUE
Architect: Douglas C. Wright Architects
Builder: Zen Restoration
Photographer: Richard Powers
Styling: Anita Sarsidi

243

MAJESTIC IN THE MOUNTAINS
Photographer: Nicolas Matheus

CONTEMPORARY IN BROOKLINE
Architect: Shope Reno Wharton
Builder: Thoughtforms
Landscape Architect: Bruce Besse
Photographer: Tim Lenz

TRADITIONAL IN CONNECTICUT
Architect: Austin Patterson Disston
Builder: Nordic Custom Builders
Photographer: Jeff MacNamara

BESPOKE IN AUSTRIA
Architect: Gebhard Fröch Ing
Builder: Kronbichler Bau GmbH
Photographer: Rudi Wyhlidal

STUNNING IN SCARSDALE
Architect: Rosamund A. Young
Builder: Cum Laude Group
Photographer: Tim Lenz

REFINED IN GREENWICH
Architect: Jones Byrne Margeotes Partners
Builder: JNC Incorporated
Landscape Architect: Renée Byers Landscape Architect, P.C.
Photographer: Tim Lenz

STREAMLINED IN THE AIR
Builder: Bombardier
Photographer: Anastassios Mentis

LUXURIOUS ON A YACHT
Builder: Composite Works

acknowledgments

To our clients, truly patrons of the creative arts. They have allowed me to stretch my imagination and expand the spectrum of my design influences. Bringing a wide array of opportunities (often disguised as design challenges), they have trusted the firm to interpret their dreams.

To my team—the firm's secret weapon of endless inspiration, myriad design solutions, and priceless camaraderie. Thank you to Marly Pena, Stephanie Daniels, Larry Bilotti, Catherine Higham, Elina Stark, Dalton Scott, Chelsea Unsworth, and Ruu Silverman. Thank you, Missy Fink, for guiding the business and supporting me and finally, Zuni Madea, our Vice President, for fifteen years of learning and growing together. Every day I am motivated by your passionate commitment to improving the quality of life through beautiful design.

To Mary Foley for believing in our vision and helping establish the foundation of the firm, to Tricia Foley for her deft hand on the text, and to Elizabeth White at Monacelli for her invaluable investment of guiding and editing this book. Thanks to Tom Maciag for envisioning and shaping the imagery to tell our story. Pam Jaccarino's generous words are a gift.

To all our industry partners, collaborators, and friends—the shared creative energy and friendship makes me look forward to the next decades of imaginative design.

And lastly, and definitely most importantly, endless thanks to my family and second family of friends who have encouraged when I hesitated and believed when I doubted.

Copyright © 2023 Foley & Cox and The Monacelli Press, a division of Phaidon Press, Inc.

First published in the United States. All rights reserved.

Library of Congress Control Number: 2022947332
ISBN 978-158093-616-3

Design: Tom Maciag and Glen Volpe, Dyad

Printed in China

Monacelli
A Phaidon Company
65 Bleecker Street
New York, New York 10012